The Small Book of

Coincidences.

(a collection of stories that seem so unreal

but are true.)

E. Byrd

ISBN –10-1721822658
ISBN-13: 978-1721822652

DEDICATION

Lots of love forever:

Daniel Byrd

Amanda Byrd

Corlis Byrd

CONTENTS

INTRODUCTION

No longer living in Clayton California with my former fiancée and our child, I find myself with a lot of spare time on my hands. I had already written two books for the people of Clayton, one is a folklore book and the other is memoirs of locals. For whatever reason, I was drawn to a new form of paranormal, not that of ghosts or even Bigfoot, but more of unusual coincidences. I have experienced a few unusual coincidences over my 52 years of life, but this book is not about myself but is about people throughout the world that have made the news due to a sequence of events that seem almost impossible to happen. I have tried to follow up on all the stories to confirm they are not just attention getters from the internet. Whenever possible, I offer you as close to the truth as I can determine.

Designed for "bathroom reading", these are very short accounts of the unusual. A small book that can be stored on a bathroom shelf. Ideal if the battery in your cell phone dies.

So, let's get started with a few well known or famous cases of the coincidence phenomenon.

Sometimes people will substitute the word "coincidence" for "conspiracy". This is often in the case of the Twin Tower attacks, but the is no conspiracy when a person is struck by lightning four times in his life. The stories attached can be deciphered in more than one way with a slight shift in mindset. Most of the coincidences are comical in nature, while other people may dig deeper into the stories and see that they are not quite so funny. Towards the end of the book, I have included a series of short internet stories that leave the results of the acts open to interpretation by the reader. Make your own conclusions. And as I have said in every book I have written. All stories have been collected from many sources and I own no rights to any of these stories. SO PLEASE DON'T SHOOT THE MESSENGER !

COINCEDENCES

[1]/ Back in 1835, a baby boy was born in Florida, Missouri as

 one of seven children. The young child was given the name Samuel Langhorne Clemens, but what was unusual about the day of Samuel's birth was the fact that it was on that day was the first appearance of Halley's Comet. After many years of success in his life, Samuel predicted that the next time the comet returns would be his last day on this Earth *"I came in with Halley's Comet in 1835. It is coming again next year, and I expect to go out with it. It will be the greatest disappointment of my life if I don't go out with Halley's Comet."*

Was it a coincidence that the man died of a heart attack on the day of Halley's Comet next appearance on April 21, 1910 in Redding, Connecticut.

Upon hearing of the death of Samuel Langhorne Clemens, President William Howard Taft said: *"This man gave pleasure – real intellectual enjoyment – to millions, and his works will continue to give such pleasure to millions yet to come ... His humor was American, but he was nearly as much appreciated by Englishmen and people of other countries as by his own*

1

countrymen. He has made an enduring part of American literature." This man who was the center of this very unusual coincidence was no other than Mark Twain. [1]

[2]/ Morgan Robertson was the son of a ship captain on

the Great Lakes. Morgan was destined to be a cabin boy and entering the merchant service when old enough. With failing vision, Morgan turned to writing fictional sea tales based on some of his experiences while on the water. After many years of rejections from local newspapers, he caught a break when a story was excepted in the *Saturday Evening Post*. Even though he never made much money from his writing but kept pushing ahead. In 1898 Robertson wrote the story entitled "Futility". Is new story describing the maiden voyage of a transatlantic luxury liner named the "Titan". The imaginary tale tells of a ship that was designed to be unsinkable and would travel the Atlantic Ocean with wealthy passengers. But after traveling for many days, and during the foggy voyage, the "Titan" strikes an iceberg and sinks with much loss of life.

Moving ahead 14 years and his book had been forgotten by most readers and 3500 miles away a ship was being built in the Belfast Harbor in 1912. Two luxury liners were being constructed, one named the Olympic and the other, the Titanic. As everyone knows, the transatlantic luxury liner widely touted as unsinkable strikes an iceberg and sinks with this great loss of life on her maiden voyage. In Morgan Robertson's book, the month of the wreck was April, same as in the real event. There were 3,000 passengers on the book; 2,207 were on the maiden voyage of the Titanic. In the book "Futility", there were 24 Lifeboats; there were 20 lifeboats on the Titanic. Most people think this is the end of the coincidence, but that is not the case.

Months after the Titanic disaster, a steamer ship was traveling through the foggy Atlantic with only a young boy on watch at the front of the ship. While daydreaming as the ship slowly made its way in the murkiness, it came into the boy's head that it had been thereabouts that the Titanic had sunk, and he was suddenly terrified by the thought of the name of his ship – the Titanian. Panic-stricken with his imagination running wild, he sounded the warning bell and whistle. Immediately, the captain on the bridge slammed the ship into reverse and slowly the ship came to a halt. Calling out from the bridge, the captain asked what the boy had seen. In a case of fear, the boy said it was a false alarm. The disgruntled captain, returned to start up the ship and continue the journey, just as within viewing distance appeared a huge iceberg loomed out of the fog directly in their path. The Titanian was saved by the boy's imagination. [2]

[3]/ Edwin Booth, is today known as the brother of assassin

 John Wilkes Booth. But during the civil war period and before the assassination, Edwin was once known as the greatest actor in American history. His reputation as an actor was described as "mythic," and a statue of him stands in Manhattan's Gramercy Park to this very day.

Edwin Booth performed a heroic act during the last months of the Civil War at a crowded train station in Jersey City. A young man who was on the same platform as Edwin Booth that day later wrote about what had happened to him in the following letter:

"The incident occurred while a group of passengers were late at night purchasing their sleeping car places from the conductor who stood on the station platform. ... There was some crowding, and I happened to be pressed by it against the car body while waiting my turn. In this situation the train began to move, and by the motion I was twisted off my feet, and had dropped somewhat, with feet downward, into the open space, and was personally helpless, when my coat collar was vigorously seized, and I was quickly pulled up

and out to a secure footing on the platform. Upon turning to thank my rescuer I saw it was Edwin Booth, whose face was of course well known to me, and I expressed my gratitude to him, and in doing so, called him by name."

Edwin Booth did the good deed, but most humans would have done the same. But Edwin genuinely had no idea who he'd just saved from a certain death. He simply accepted the child's gratitude, signed him an autograph, and spent the rest of his afternoon on a train heading to his next port of call. It was a few days later, Edwin Booth received a letter of commendation from Adam Badeau, an officer to the staff of General Ulysses S. Grant. It turned out that the young man Edwin had saved was Robert Todd Lincoln, the son of President Abraham Lincoln who was assassinated a year later by Edwin's brother, John Wilkes Booth. [3]

[4]/ Born Violet Constance Jessop in Argentina. The first child

of Irish emigrant with her other five siblings. Violet moved to England with her mother and the other children after her father's death. After attending school, Violet Jessop became an ocean liner stewardess. But was Violet a jinx? The reason was that Violet survived three separate disasters on

Olympic-class ocean liners, including the sinking of the *RMS Titanic*.

Jessop was on the *RMS Olympic* on its fifth voyage on 20 September 1911 when the boat crashed with the cruiser, *HMS Hawke*. At the time of the accident, the *Olympic* was the largest civilian liner in the world. *RMS Olympic* took heavy damage and flooding in the crash but was able to make it back to Southampton, UK to be repaired.

Seven months later, on April 10, 1912, Violet boarded the *RMS Titanic* on the ship's maiden voyage. Four days later, the boat hit an iceberg and sank in the North Atlantic. After helping many people get off of the ship, she was able to board the 16th lifeboat and was handed a baby to look after as the lifeboat was lowered in the icy water. Once rescue ships arrived, Violet, the baby and the other women in the lifeboat were all pulled to safety.

After the outbreak of World War I, Jessop worked as a stewardess for the British Red Cross. On November 21, 1916, she was onboard the *HMHS Britannic* when the ship hit a mine and sank in the Aegean located between Greece and Turkey. The *Britannic* was the largest ship to be lost during World War I, and 30 people died in the tragedy. Before the *Britannic* was lost under the waves, Jessop made sure to grab her toothbrush because it was the one item she most missed in the aftermath of her *Titanic* experience. [4]

[5] / In 1966 The Beatles released the album *Revolver*. On this album, track #2 on side 1 is a song about lonely people in their respective towns throughout the country. "Eleanor Rigby" was released by The Beatles on August 5, 1966, Ranked 137 on Rolling Stone's top

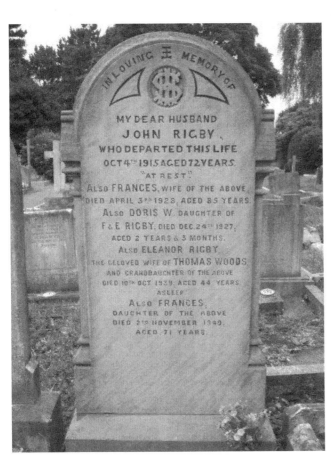

500 greatest songs of all-time list. The song was not just on the album, but also as a single 45rpm with *"Yellow Submarine"*. With the success of the album, Paul McCartney gave an interview about how he came up with the song. He said that he came up with the idea from looking in the phone book and found "McKenzie." Ultimately, the name "Father McKenzie" was used in the song's lyrics. McCartney came up with the name "Eleanor" from actress

Eleanor Bron and "Rigby" from a store in Bristol named Rigby & Evens Ltd, Wine & Spirit Shippers. In 1984.

It was in the 1980s, that a grave was discovered in St. Peter's Parish Church in Liverpool, with the name Eleanor Rigby on it. Even more, coincidentally, a few yards from Eleanor's grave is another tombstone with the last name "McKenzie" on it. The cemetery is located near the spot where Lennon and McCartney first met, and the two spent a lot of time in the cemetery as young friends. [5]

[6]/ In 1914, WWI had only just begun, and two former  civilian steamships, fitted out for war, fought to the death. SMS *Cap Trafalgar*, an ocean liner. She was 613 feet long, and 72 wide, the largest commercial ship in South American waters. The SMS *Cap Trafalgar* in Uruguay waters was converted to a warship. While in Bermuda, the RMS *Carmania* was going through the same conversion as its counterpart. The RMS *Carmania* 653 feet long, cruised a knot faster than the SMS *Cap Trafalgar* and was armed with eight, 4.7-inch quick firing guns. It was on September 14, 1914, these two ships would fight to the death when their paths crossed on the open seas.

The *Cap Trafalgar* was on patrol near Trindade Island, Brazil, where the Imperial German Navy had established a supply base. The *Carmania* knew where the German ship was operating. She approached the small Island around 11 am on September 14, 1914.

It was about an hour later, the *Carmania* could see The *Cap Trafalgar* at first, the *Carmania's* captain seemed confused; her prey was painted almost identically to her. There was no reason for a fellow British ship to be in this area unreported, and the ship was on a rapid retreat. This seemed unusual, and communication was attempted, but no British ships were in the vicinity, so she pursued the unknown ship. After a short chase, the *Cap Trafalgar* turned to bear down on the *Carmania*. At 8,500 yards, the *Carmania* fired the first shot. The *Cap Trafalgar* responded almost immediately with gunfire.

The *Carmania* scored a hit in the *Cap Trafalgar's* bow starting a fire and causing her to list. Then the *Carmania's* forward cabin caught fire. Both ships continued the fight. The *Cap Trafalgar* continued to fire onto *Carmania's* decks.
The *Carmania,* changed her aim to *Cap Trafalgar* blasting holes in the ship's side, leaning to her crew filling the lifeboats. With the *Carmania* barely afloat, she listed severely as fires burned on her desks.

The battle had lasted less than 2 hours, cost the lives of approximately 60 men out of the 600 aboard the ships. To make the most of their naval warfare, both the British and the German navies disguised battleships as passenger ships. In a chance encounter, the British ship RMS Carmania, which had been disguised as the German passenger ship SMS Cap Trafalgar, met and sank the German raider SMS Cap Trafalgar which had been disguised as the British RMS Carmania. [6]

[7] / In 1837, Edgar Allen Poe wrote his first and only full-

length novel "The Narrative of Arthur Gorden Pym of Nantucket." The gruesome story is about a young boy named Arthur Gorden Pym who stows away on a ship in search of adventure. One part of the novel tells how the ship sank and the crew had to survive off of captured turtle. When the meat ran out, they were forced to pulling straws to see who would be cannibalized, so the rest of the crew could survive. A young cabin boy named Richard Parker pulled the short straw leading to his execution.

Forty-six years later, a ship named the Mignonette left England for Australia. The ship sank in a storm, and the crew who was able to escape the sinking ship, survived off turtle meat captured on the small island they had found themselves. When the turtle meat ran out, the crew were starving and near death. It was then that it was decided to draw straws to see who would be killed and eaten. The young cabin boy pulled the short straw and was soon cannibalized. His name was Richard Parker. [7]

[8] / In April 1865, Robert Todd Lincoln resigned his U.S.

Army commission and moved to Chicago with his mother. He later married, had children and established a successful law practice. He accepts the post of secretary of war in the administration of President James A. Garfield in 1881. It was July 1881, Lincoln was at the railroad station in Washington, ready to travel to New Jersey with President Garfield. Before their departure, a drifter named Charles Guiteau shot the newly inaugurated President James A. Garfield in the back. Garfield managed to live on for 80 more days, but a severe infection eventually led to his death.

Moving ahead, in 1901, President William McKinley invited Lincoln to Buffalo, New York to attend the Pan-American Exposition. This event had worried President William McKinley staff members, some of whom feared that an assassin might take the opportunity to strike. The president's personal secretary, George B. Cortelyou, had even tried to cancel the reception on two separate occasions in the meantime, Lincoln arrived on the afternoon of September 6, 1901, heading to meet the president. As

Lincoln arrived, standing near the front of the line to witness the president in person stood 28-year-old Leon Czolgosz, a former steelworker, and an anarchist. He waited with the gun wrapped in a white handkerchief and concealed inside his jacket pocket. "It was in my heart; there was no escape for me," Czolgosz later said. "All those people seemed to bow to the great ruler. I made up my mind to kill that ruler."

Czolgosz walked up to the president at around 4:07 p.m. Czolgosz raised his pistol, still wrapped in its white handkerchief, and fired two shots at point-blank range. "There was an instant of almost complete silence, like the hush that follows a clap of thunder," the New York Times wrote. "The president stood stock still, a look of hesitancy, almost of bewilderment, on his face. Then he retreated a step while a pallor began to steal over his features. The multitude seemed only partially aware that something serious had happened."

An African American man named James "Big Jim" Parker who had been waiting in line to meet the president, punched Czolgosz and prevented him from firing a third shot Robert Lincoln witnessed the whole event, bring back memories of his father's demise. McKinley was taken to a hospital and underwent emergency surgery, but he later developed gangrene and blood poisoning. He would die eight days after the shooting, becoming the third U.S. president to fall victim to an assassin's bullet and all three were witnessed by Robert Lincoln. [8]

[9] / On June 28, 1914, in Sarajevo, a coincidence took place

that would change the world forever. Gavrilo Princip and some of his other Serbian nationalists were on the streets of Sarajevo waiting for Archduke Franz Ferdinand motorcade to pass by. While in power, the Archduke attempted to restore Austro-Russian relations while maintaining an alliance with Germany. Archduke Franz Ferdinand's public persona was cold, sharped-tongued and short-tempered. He was also rumored to be insane due to the inbreeding of his family.

In the summer of 1914, Franz Ferdinand and wife Sophie accepted an invitation to visit the capital of Bosnia, Sarajevo. He had been informed of terrorist activity conducted by the nationalist organization the "Black Hand," but ignored the warnings. On the morning of June 28, 1914, the royal couple arrived by train and a six-car motorcade drove them to city hall for an official reception.

As the motorcade passed the central police station, a Black Hand agent, Nedjelko Cabrinovic, tossed a hand grenade at the archduke's car. The driver accelerated when he saw the flying object, and the bomb exploded underneath the wheel of the next car, injuring two of its occupants along with a dozen spectators.

Meanwhile, Gavrilo took off running with the crowd. He was

so upset and infuriated that their plan didn't work out he went to a coffee shop to calm his thoughts and try and understand why the plot had failed. After finishing his drink and regaining his composure after the failed attempt on the Archduke, Gavrilo exits the coffee shop only to see the motorcade heading his way. The motorcade was on the route back to the palace, the archduke's driver took a wrong turn into a side street which led right past his current location. The driver had realized his mistake and pulled the car to a halt and put the vehicle in reverse. Slowly the car started to move backward and out of the back street. Gavrilo saw an opportunity and quickly walked over towards the approaching car. Reaching inside his jacket, pulling out a pistol, cocked the gun, raised his arm and fired, striking Sophie in the abdomen and the Archduke in the neck. After the shots were fired, the car sped off and instead of heading to the palace, the new location was the hospital. Both died before reaching their destination.

This coincidence changed the world and caused millions of people to die over the next few years. The reason for this is that the assassination of Archduke Franz Ferdinand gave the hardliners in Austria-Hungary the opportunity to act against Serbia and put an end to their fight for independence. In July 1914, Austria-Hungary declared war against Serbia. As was expected, the complex web of alliances was activated as Russia declared war on Austria-Hungary, Germany declared war on Russia, and France and Britain declared war on Germany and Austria-Hungary. Which is now known as the outbreak of World War I. [9]

[10] / Since James Dean's death in 1955, the Porsche 550

Spyder has become infamous as the car that killed him. While filming *Rebel Without A Cause*, James Dean purchased the 550 Spyder and decided he wanted to customize the car to his specifications. The car was giving tartan seats, two red stripes over the rear wheels and plastered the number '130' on its doors, hood and engine cover. The name "<u>Little Bastard</u>" was later painted on the car. On September 23 of 1955, Dean met actor Alec Guinness outside of a restaurant and had him look at the Spyder. Guinness told Dean that the car had a "sinister" appearance and then told Dean: "If you get in that car, you will be found dead in it by this time next week." A week later, Dean would be killed at the Intersection of 41 & 46 in Cholame, CA.

The car named "Little Bastard" was supposed to be cursed.

George Barris, who customized the 550 originally, bought the wrecked carcass of "Little Bastard" for $2500 and soon after it slipped off its trailer

15

and broke a mechanics leg. Not feeling good about the car, the 550 parts were sold to Troy McHenry and William Eschrid. While the two were both racing against one another in cars that had parts from the "Little Bastard," McHenry lost control and hit a tree, killing him instantly and Eschrid was seriously injured when his car suddenly locked up and rolled over while going into a turn.

Two tires from the were, but soon after the sale both blew out simultaneously causing the new owner's car to run off the road. Two would-be thieves broke into the garage where the remaining parts sat but one of the thief's arms was torn open trying to steal the steering wheel while the other was injured trying to remove the bloodstained tartan seat. The California Highway Patrol asked to use the car in an exhibit they were hosting. The first exhibit was unsuccessful as the garage that housed the car caught fire and burned to the ground. Mysteriously the car suffered virtually no damage from the fire. The car was removed from the burnt-out building and was transported to a local high school. This display did not last long because the car fell off its display and broke a student's hip.

When you think things could not get any worse, the curse continued when the "Little Bastard" was being transported when the truck carrying the car lost control which caused the driver to fall out of the cab of the truck and somehow get crushed by the car after it fell off the back. This series of unlucky events seem impossible, but it is not over yet. The car fell off not one but two more transport trucks while traveling on the freeway fortunately not injuring anyone. The CHP decided that it had had enough of the "Little Bastard" and while transporting the car to its owner, the car mysteriously vanished and has not been seen since. [10]

[11] / During the summer of 1861, Wilmer McLean and his

family were living on a plantation near Manassas Junction, Virginia. As Union forces approached, Confederate General P.G.T. Beauregard took over the farm as his headquarters. On July 21, 1861, the first major battle of the Civil War took place at Bull Run as well as the second Battle of Bull Run which took place 13 months later., which ran through McLean's property.

As the war continued around the families plantation, in 1863, McLean and his family had relocated to the small hamlet of Appomattox Court House, some 120 miles away. McLean, who supplied sugar to the Confederate Army, was in Appomattox on April 9, 1865, when Confederate Colonel Charles Marshal approached him for assistance finding a suitable place to host a meeting between General Robert E. Lee and his Union counterpart, Ulysses S. Grant. It was that day that Lee surrendered to Grant in McLean's parlor.

[12] / Johann Wolfgang von Goethe (1749-1832) was a

 famous German writer, poet, and politician. One day, a depressed Goethe was riding on a footpath after visiting a friend named Frederika. Suddenly, he faced a mysterious person riding toward him. The person, who Goethe said he saw with a "mind's eye" instead of his actual eyes, was clearly Goethe himself, although he was wearing different clothes. The figure soon disappeared from sight, and Goethe soon forgot all about what he thought he had seen.

Eight years later while heading to see his same friend, he found himself riding down the same footpath in the opposite direction. That's when he realized he was wearing the exact same clothes his doppelganger wore years ago. This was not the only doppelganger Goethe saw. Another time, he saw his friend Friedrich walking on the street, wearing Goethe's own dressing gown. Puzzled, Goethe went home only to find Friedrich there, wearing the same gown Goethe had seen on the apparition. His friend had been surprised by the rain and borrowed the gown as his clothes dried.

[13] / George Edwin Ellison and John Henry Parr have the

 misfortune to share a very rare distinction and final resting place. George Edwin Ellison (1878 – 11 November 1918)

was the last British soldier to be killed in action during the First World War. He died at 09:30 am (90 minutes before the armistice came into effect) while on a patrol on the outskirts of Mons. Sometime just before the outbreak of war, he was recalled to the army, joining the 5th Royal Irish Lancers, serving in the army at the start of the war.

Private John Henry Parr (19 July 1897 – 21 August 1914) was a British soldier who was believed to be the first soldier of the British Commonwealth to be killed by enemy action in the First World War. Private Parr specialized in becoming a reconnaissance cyclist, riding ahead to uncover information then returning with all possible speed to update the commanding officer. It is believed that they encountered the German First Army and that Parr remained to hold off the enemy whilst his companion returned to report. He was killed in the ensuing rifle fire.

So, what is the coincidence between these two British soldiers that seem to have nothing in common but being the first and last man killed in the war? the coincidences come from the location where these two men are buried. They are both buried in the St Symphorien Military Cemetery, Mons France. Coincidentally, the two graves face each other with only 15 feet between them. [13]

[14] / In 1885, John "Babbacombe" Lee was convicted of the  murder of Emma Keyse, at her home at Babbacombe Bay in England. The evidence against Lee was weak, amounting to little more than Lee has been the only male in the house at the time of the murder. Despite this and his claim of innocence, he was sentenced to hang. When he was taken back to jail, he said he had not killed the woman and pleaded his innocence. When the governor and the chaplain left the cell later that evening, Lee settled down and had no difficulty sleeping. Lee later said that he dreamed he was standing on the gallows with the noose around his neck, but the trapdoor wouldn't open, despite the repeated yanks the hangman was giving to the lever. When Lee awoke from the dream, he felt that God had assured him that there was nothing to worry about, as he would not die on the gallows.

Shortly before eight o'clock on the morning of Monday, 23rd February 1885, John Lee was led to the gallows and the rope was tightened around his neck. The white hood was pulled over Lee's head, and then he waited for the click of the lever and a split second later, his neck would snap as his body weight pulled tightly on the rope. After a short tense pause, the trap door on which John Lee stood refused to open. Had Lee's dream come true?

The hood and noose were removed from Lee and he was led aside. The hangman tested the strap with a sandbag that weighed the exact same weight as Lee. The trap opened this time and the sandbag crashed to the ground under the gallows. Lee was moved back into position over the trap door. Once more, the hood was placed over his head and the noose re-positioned around his neck.

With an almost guarantee that the glitch had been fixed, the lever was pulled for the second time. The sound of the bolts releasing and for a split second, Lee thought this was the last breath he would ever breathe - but the trap beneath Lee's feet wouldn't open for the second time. For a second time, the noose and hood were removed and Lee and guided off the trap. Not knowing what to do next, the hangman called in a prison engineer to discuss the jamming problem. It was decided that a prisoner /carpenter to be summoned to make needed alterations to the trap door itself. When the edges of the trap had been filed down, and the bolts of the hanging apparatus had been greased, a sandbag acted as a substitute for Lee again. The test runs worked just fine, and it was decided that they would try once again to hang Lee. Lee was put on the trap for the third time and the hooded man stood there, waiting for the lever to be thrown for what had to be the last time. Mr. Berry, the hangman pulled the lever as hard as possible.

The greased bolts slid as expected. But Lee was still standing on the unopened trap. Lee was granted a respite by the Home Secretary, with the death sentence had been commuted to life imprisonment. Lee was released after serving twenty years. John Lee, the man who couldn't be hanged, swore he was not a murderer. Whenever people asked him what he thought about being spared from the rope three times in a row, Lee would say it wasn't luck or freak mechanical failure that saved his neck - but divine intervention. [14]

[15] / In 1938, the well-known diplomat and author Sir Harold

George published a strange story told him by a friend. Prince Otto von Bismarck of Prussia, was attacked by a lone gunman named Ferdinand Cohen-Blind on May 7, 1866, and famously fought the assassin to a standstill even as the gunman was still trying to shoot him. Five shots were fired with three missing the target, one bullet grazing Bismarck's shoulder, and the other ricocheting off of one of Bismarck's ribs. According to Nicolson's friend Leopold the failed assassins confiscated possessions were auctioned off by the police. A friend of Bismarck's named Delbrück bought the gun at the auction and then presented it to the Prince as a gift.

Twenty years later, in 1886, Leopold's father was visiting. They had just had lunch, and Bismarck and the men of the group had retired to the smoking-room to relax. The ladies were being given a tour of the home. As the tour reached Bismarck's study, the Princess announced: "and this is the pistol which Blind used in 1866." A moment later, the gun discharged. Luckily no one was hurt, but Bismarck was very upset that people would handle such an important collector's item. He stated that no-one must be allowed to touch it ever again! And yet, the weapon remained on display in Bismarck's study.

Moving forward to 1906 that Nicolson's friend Leopold himself was staying at Bismarck's home with a collection of other family members. On a tour of the home, Leopold showed them the study where the revolver sat on display. Leopold told the visitors the story of how the revolver had been accidentally triggered twenty years after the 1866 assassination attempt while his father was visiting, showing them how it had been handled when the gun once again fired, lodging the sixth bullet from Blind's gun in Leopold's bicep. [15]

[16] /Born in 1841, Charles Francis Coghlan was raised and

 educated in both Paris, France, and London, England and despite his parents' hope that he would become a lawyer, he had an interest and was honing his natural talent for both writing and acting. His first appearance upon the stage was at 19 years old back in 1860. His ability to learn the characters so well and his entertaining personality, by 1862, he was playing the lead roles throughout England and France.

Over the next 37 years, Charles Coghlan became well renowned for his acting talent on tours throughout Europe and North America. Many times, the call of the stage called him back out for just one more set of performances. But Coghlan's health took a distinct turn for the worse leading to his death on November 27.

He was given a beautiful metal coffin and temporarily interred at a local cemetery to await his final resting spot. Mother Nature decided the matter for everyone on September 8, 1900, when Galveston was nearly destroyed by a hurricane along with the local graveyard, washing many caskets out to sea including the casket of Charles Coghlan.

Charles Coghlan's wandering coffin did eventually turn up again, and in a surprising place: years after the hurricane, the metal coffin of Charles Coghlan -- apparently airtight enough to float --

was washed ashore on Prince Edward Island, not far from his home. I am not sure I can personally believe this statement.

Two books by other people involved in the world of the theater at the time that Coghlan died, though only one of the two mentions this legend.

Sir Johnston Forbes-Robertson, an English actor and theater manager who published his memoirs -- *A Player Under Three Reigns* -- in 1925.

"Shortly after his burial there a great storm came up from the Gulf which swept his [Coghlan's] coffin with others into the sea. The Gulf Stream bore him round Florida, up the coast about fifteen hundred miles to Prince Edward Island, and he came ashore not far from his home."

The other memoir, *The Days I Knew*, by actress Lillie Langtry and published in 1925 though there is no good reason he included it. Here's what she tells us about Charles Coghlan:

"He died and was buried at Galveston, Texas, but his remains were not allowed to rest in peace, for the tidal wave that later demolished that town invaded the cemetery and swept many of the coffins (including that of Charles Coghlan) out to sea, which singular happening to his remains was predicted for him by a crystal-gazer while he was still a young man!"

On September 27, 1900, it was reported that Coghlan's casket was found sixteen miles north of Galveston, near the town of La Marque; the undertaker who first placed the casket in the vault in Galveston was on his way to La Marque to identify the remains.

Then many years later on January 22, 1904, it was reported that a
metallic casket believed to belong to Coghlan had been found on
the beach near Galveston. Only 3 years later in 1907, it was
reported that Coghlan's metal coffin had been found almost buried
in a marsh, hidden by weeds about nine miles from Galveston. Still
not content with the outcome of the coffin's location, it was
reported in 1909, a memoir was written by Squire and Marie Effie
Bancroft, theater actors and managers, stated that Coghlan's coffin
had been found floating on the ocean "sometime afterwards" of the
hurricane, and been reburied keeping in mind it hadn't been buried
before. The legend seemed to have come to an end with a nine-
year hiatus from public reports of its sighting, but in April 1918,
Lillie Langtry first made the claim that a "crystal-gazer" had
foreseen the fate of Coghlan's remains when he was a young man,
a claim she repeated in her memoirs later. But with all the
confusion about the famous moving coffin, it was in June 1922, an
article about Rose Coghlan, Charles Coghlan's sister who was also
an actress, it is stated that the iron coffin of her brother was never
recovered. [16]

[17] / Both John Adams and Thomas Jefferson had been

central in the drafting of
the Declaration of
Independence along with
the other well-known
representatives; Jefferson
had authored it, and

Adams, who was known as the "colossus of the debate," served on the drafting committee and had argued eloquently for the declaration's passage. The 4th of July was to be a huge milestone for America, by remarkable coincidence, Jefferson and Adams died on the same day, Independence Day in 1826, the 50th anniversary of the adoption of the Declaration of Independence. Three of the five Founding Father Presidents died on the Independence Day anniversary. Back on July 4, 1831, James Monroe, the fifth President succumb on that same day.

In 1831, the *New York Evening Post* called it a "coincidence

that has no parallel." "Three of the four presidents who have left the scene of their usefulness and glory expired on the anniversary of the national birthday, a day which of all others, had it been permitted them to choose they would probably had selected for the termination of their careers," the *Post* reported. The Frederick, Maryland *Town Herald,* the New York *Commercial,* the *Boston Traveler Advertiser,* New York's *Journal of Commerce* marked Monroe's passing on July 9, 1831 by also noting the "presidential coincidence."

[18] / Over a three-day period between June 22 and June 24,

2007, Chris Benoit, a 40-year-old veteran professional wrestler employed by World Wrestling Entertainment (WW E), killed his wife Nancy Benoit and strangled their 7-year-old son Daniel before hanging himself. Autopsy results showed that Benoit's wife was murdered first as she was bound at the feet and wrists and died of asphyxiation on the June 22.

The couple's son, Daniel Christopher Benoit, also died of asphyxia, apparently killed as he lay in bed on the morning of June 23. Then on the evening of June 24, Benoit died by suicide in his weight room, when he used a weight lifting machine to break his own neck.

The coincidence came 14 hours before their bodies were discovered by police when Benoit's Wikipedia page was updated to say that he'd been having difficulties because of "personal issues ... stemming from the death of his wife Nancy." The edit was reversed within the hour because there was no sourcing information, and the trolls, who were determined to continue with the joke that a normal person would realize isn't funny under any circumstances, reposted the claim with sourcing attributed to "several pro wrestling websites."

The first "hacker" came from Stamford, Connecticut, which also happens to be WWE headquarters, and the second came from Sydney, Australia. Atlanta police were informed about the edits and ultimately investigated the Benoit home after the WWE received some unsettling text messages. The Wiki user declined all interviews but did post an apology saying that the entire thing was "just a major coincidence" and that he'd made the random assertion on his own, just as a joke. [18]

[19] / November 9 was a very memorable date in the Nazi

party. Starting in 1848 with the execution of Robert Blum, a crusader for establishing democracy throughout the German-speaking world. Fast-forward to 1918, and Germany's first democracy, the Weimar Republic, was established. 1923, Hitler and his followers tried to overthrow the Weimar Republic with their Bierkellerputsch, and while that failed, two years later, in 1925, Hitler founded the elite SS force. The Nazi's most notorious date comes on November 9, 1938. Known as Kristallnacht ("Night of Broken Glass") when the Nazis unleashed a reign of terror on Jews across the country. 1989, The fall of the Berlin Wall .[19]

[20] You may not want to go on vacation with Jason and

Jenny Cairns-Lawrence of Birmingham UK. Jason and Jenny Cairns-Lawrence were vacationing in New York City on September 11, 2001. the day of the terrorist attacks on the World Trade Center. They weren't among the thousands of casualties, but when it came time to pick their next vacation, they decided to stay a little closer home. They chose London, and on July 7, 2005, they were in the nation's capital when four suicide bombers killed dozens and injured hundreds of people on the London Underground. With all the problems the couple seemed to follow them around, that did not stop them. 2008, they were faced with making a vacation choice again. They headed to Mumbai, and they were staying in the Colaba area when terrorists attacked the city on November 26, killing almost 180 people. In a horrible series of coincidences. [20]

[21] / Leonard Dawe was just an ordinary guy with an

ordinary job. He was the headmaster of the Strand School in Surrey, and he had one of the most seemingly harmless hobbies ever: he liked crosswords. His hobby led to him writing them for The Telegraph. In June 1944, MI5 showed up at his place of work and was escorted into a car and driven away. It was a few days later that he reappeared but refusing to say a word about what happened.

The reason Dawe's was taken into custody an MI5 officer was trying to take his mind off his work during a lunch break by doing a little crossword puzzle-solving. As the crossword puzzle started to fill out, the MI5 officer started to get concerned when he started finding words like "Mulberry", "Overlord," "Juno," "Omaha," "Neptune," and "Utah," in the puzzle. All the words were connected to the super top-secret code words for various parts of the D-Day plan. The officer thought that the war plan was being passed to spies and what would prevent from the final days of the war.

It turned out that Dawe wrote his crossword by giving his students in his class a blank layout, asking them to fill in the words, and then writing the clues to the words they had written in the blank spots. Unfortunately for him, the boys had been hanging out with some soldiers stationed nearby, and they had written down some of the cool words that they'd overheard. [21]

[22] / Leslie Parker, a teenager living in Tampa, Florida gave

birth to a girl. A year later, she gave birth to another girl, and both were given up for adoption. The elder daughter was named

Lizzie Valverde and grew up in New Jersey. The second daughter was named Katy Olson and grew up in Iowa.

Both women moved to New York City and enrolled in Columbia University's School of General Studies. Once enrolled, the two women signed up for the same literary reporting class. At the beginning of the class in January 2013, the instructor had the students introduce themselves, and Valverde explained that she was adopted, that she was from Florida, and began to share a few other pieces of personal information with the class. Almost immediately, Olson knew that there could be a connection between both females.

The two women made a point to meet after class and immediately started sharing their lives with each other. It was then that they knew they were sisters. They are close now and have even gotten in contact with their birth mother.[22]

[23] / Daniel Stefanus du Toit was born in Springfontein, in

South Africa, on 15 December 1917, his education led him to the Boyden Observatory (Harvard College Observatory, Boyden station) at Maselspoort in 1936. After many years of hard work and research, he became the chief assistant to the director Dr. John S. Paraskevopoulos.

During his time with Dr.

Paraskevopoulos, he discovered and co-discovered several comets. Daniel left the observatory after the war to pursue a career in the building industry. Due to an accident that left Daniel with a severe leg injury, he was forced into early retirement. Needing to find another career, and with the eventual loss of the leg, he started doing a series of speeches and talks on his discoveries and the meaning of life in space and time. He was invited to speak at Free State University in Bloemfontein, South Africa. Nothing out of the ordinary was spoken of that evening. He discussed the comets he had discovered He climbs to the pedestal and proceeds to lecture on the sciences and the meaning of life. But for some reason, he finished his speech with a statement that was not normally said during his talks. He said "who knows how long we will all survive on this plant. There is a chance we could die and any second". With a huge round of applause, du Toit takes a bow, thanks the audience and walks off the stage. Knowing that he would be required to answer many questions from behind the curtain when he was stood in the wings of the theater, he reached into his pocket and pulled out a mint to help freshen his breath before meeting the staff of the university. It was then that du Toit chocked on the mint and was unable to dislodge it. Collapsing to the floor, Daniel du Toit died on the spot, not moments after saying you could die at any time. [23]

[24] / "The Taking of the City of Washington by the British

 Forces Under Major General Ross on August 24, 1814... the public property destroyed amounted to thirty Millions of Dollars." One hundred and ninety-six years ago today, the British sacked the District of Columbia. They were, in turn, sacked by a tornado.

In 1814, the British wanted revenge. U.S. troops had burned the legislative building, government structures, and private warehouses in the Battle of York (modern-day Toronto), and the Brits were inclined to teach their former colonies a lesson in how to properly sack a city. Their charge on the American capital city was led by British Maj. Gen. Robert Ross and Adm. George Cockburn, who burned the Capitol, the White House, the Treasury Department, and plenty of other government buildings without losing a single soldier. Cockburn was, well, a cocky fellow. Aside from burning much of the District, he did it with an unapologetic gusto. He supped on the dinner that had been prepared for President James Madison before burning down the White House.

While marching back through the city, he also made a stop at the *National Intelligencer,* where the editor had been "telling some tough stories" about him and later had all the c's removed from the press so the editor could no longer spell his name. As a testament to Cockburn's ego, when he returned to camp after burning much of the District, he left a single soldier to guard the captured city overnight. Unfortunately for Cockburn, day two of sacking the U.S. capital did not go so well. First, a dozen of his soldiers was killed when gunpowder and ammunition were accidentally ignited at modern-day Fort McNair. Then a tornado struck. While historians and meteorologists can't quite commit to whether D.C. experienced a serendipitous hurricane, tornado, tropical storm, or severe thunderstorm, they all agree that the weather turned quite nasty on the redcoats.

According to one British account of George Muller's *The Darkest Day*:

Of the prodigious force of the wind, it is impossible for you to form any conception. Roofs of houses were torn off by it and whisked into the air like sheets of paper; while the rain which accompanied it resembled the rushing of a mighty cataract rather than the dropping of a shower. The darkness was as great as if the sun had long set and the last remains of twilight had come on, occasionally relieved by flashes of vivid lightning streaming through it; which, together with the noise of the wind and the thunder, the crash of falling buildings, and the tearing of roofs as they were stripped from the walls, produced the most appalling effect I ever have, and probably ever shall, witness.

This lasted for nearly two hours without intermission, during which time many of the houses spared by us were blown down and thirty of our men, besides several of the inhabitants, buried beneath their ruins. Our column was as completely dispersed as if it had received a total defeat, some of the men flying for shelter behind walls and buildings and others falling flat upon the ground to prevent themselves from being carried away by the tempest. The storm did its damage to the city, but the deluge also helped extinguish the flames of the burning capital. The District was abandoned after just 26 hours, and the War of 1812 would stretch on until the Treaty of Ghent. As for Cockburn, his return to England in 1815 was short-lived, as he was immediately assigned the task of conveying (former) Emperor Napoleon to Saint Helena, where he served as the French ruler's jailer. [24]

[25] / In the 1950s, Stefan Lorant was researching a book on

Abraham Lincoln when he came across an image of the President's funeral procession as it moved down Broadway in New York City. The photo was dated April 25, 1865. At first, it appeared like one of any number of photographs of Lincoln's funeral procession. The photo was included in Lorant's files and future research was done. With a strange coincidence, the photo was taken across the street from Cornelius van Schaack Roosevelt's home, the grandfather of future President Teddy Roosevelt. The coincidence might have ended there, but Lorant took a closer look. In the second story window of the Roosevelt mansion, he noticed the heads of two boys peering out of the window as Lincoln's funeral procession marches by. Lorant had the rare chance to ask Teddy Roosevelt's wife about the image, and

when she saw it, she confirmed what he had suspected: the faces in the windows were those of a young future President and his brother, Elliott. "Yes, I think that is my husband, and next to him his brother," she exclaimed. "That horrible man! I was a little girl then and my governess took me to Grandfather Roosevelt's house on Broadway, so I could watch the funeral procession. But as I looked down from the window and saw all the black draping I became frightened and started to cry. Theodore and Elliott were both there. They didn't like my crying. They took me and locked me in a back room. I never did see Lincoln's funeral." [25]

[26] / In 1970 popular science-fiction author Philip K. Dick

 wrote a book titled "Flow My Tears, the Policeman Said". It took him no time at all to write as he was carried by a <u>strong inspiration</u>. He later met a woman who had the same name as one of his characters. She was the same age, and her boyfriend had the same name as the character's boyfriend. Further, she was involved in a crime ring like the character in the book but later revealed that she was having an affair with a police officer, also like the character in the book. The mystery goes further, as Dick describes in his 1978 essay titled "How to Build a Universe That Doesn't Fall Apart Two Days Later."

"One afternoon I was talking to my priest—I am an Episcopalian—and I happened to mention to him an important scene near the end of the novel in which the character Felix Buckman meets a black stranger at an all-night gas station, and they begin to talk. As I described the scene in more and more detail, my priest became progressively more agitated. At last, he said, 'That is a scene from the Book of Acts, from the Bible!'" Dick checked and found the events matched up in detail and even the names were repeated in his story and in the Bible. [26]

[27] / In the movie "Troy", Brad Pitt plays the mythical hero

Achilles, was invincible, except for one weakness - his heel. Picture that scene where Pitt, imbued with the might of Achilles, leaps in the air to take out Eric Bana, who's playing a character called Hector. If you're remembering rightly, this is the part where Hector dies - it was also the scene in which, during filming, Brad Pitt landed awkwardly and *tore his Achilles tendon. Yes, after landing he crumpled to the ground in intense pain. Medics were on the scene within seconds, but it was clear that filming would have to stop until the Achilles healed.* [27]

[28] / Making movies about things like evil spirits and the

devil is a good way to get people to say that movies are "cursed," especially if something bad happens whilst making that movie. Things like the deaths of most of your cast members in *Poltergeist*, or the entire crew ending up with cancer on the set of *The Conqueror*. *The Omen*, of course, is one of those movies believed to have been "cursed," and a coincidence is enough to scare you to death. This coincidence is terrifying but very true. During the filming of the movie, the director needed to hire a private jet for the actor's transportation needs. The rental company needed the jet it at the time the production company wanted it. An offer was made, and a discount was offered if they waited a few days. The need for the jet during the first few days was not important, so they agreed to wait a few days with a large discount on the overall cost of the rental. Later that day the private jet that was supposed to be heading to the movie set crashed onto a road and into a couple of cars that were on the road. Everybody involved in the crash was killed. The coincidence came from the wife and child of the pilot flying the jet just happened to be *inside* one of those cars hit on the freeway. [28]

[29] / Martial arts icon Jackie Chan and the shooting of a

canceled movie called *Nosebleed.* According to Chan, he was scheduled to shoot a scene inside the World Trade Center on September 11th, 2001 but decided not to because he wasn't happy with the script and pursued another project. The movie was rumored to have been about *terrorists who try to blow up the World Trade Center,* amongst other iconic buildings and monuments in New York City. He would have been strapped to the side of one the towers, given that his character was supposed to have been a window cleaner. Talking about the incident, Chan himself is quoted as having said: "Filming was scheduled to have taken place at 7:00 am on September 11th, and as I had to be at the top of one of the towers for one of the scenes, I

would probably have died if the shooting went ahead as planned."
The movie he opted to make instead, by the way, was *The Tuxedo*.

[30] / The original album cover sleeve for Lynyrd

Skynyrd's *Street Survivors* had featured a photograph of the band
standing on a city street with buildings engulfed in flames, some of
the flames near the center nearly obscuring Steve Gaines. Some
people thought this to be an omen of bad things too. When renting
an airplane to transport the band to their next gig. Concerns over
both the safety of the plane and the readiness of its crew, Lynyrd
Skynyrd boarded the plane anyhow and were traveling from
Greenville, S.C., to Baton Rouge, La. When their plane apparently
ran out of fuel toward the end of the flight. The pilots attempted to
land on a small airstrip, but the bottom of the plane clipped some
trees, and the aircraft went down in a remote stand of forest. Singer
Ronnie Van Zant, guitarist Steve Gaines, vocalist Cassie Gaines,
assistant road manager Dean Kilpatrick, pilot Walter McCreary
and co-pilot William Gray were killed instantly, while the other
band members and road crew suffered serious injuries.

After the plane crash killed several band members, the album cover became highly controversial. Out of respect of the families, MCA Records withdrew the original cover and replaced it with a similar image of the band against a simple black background, which was on the back cover of the original album. Conspiracy theorists have long been quick to point out that only those band members touched by flame in the photograph were killed in the crash.

[31] / During the Cold War years, the Hollow Nickel Case was

one of the most famous spy cases in the United States. In 1953, a newspaper boy in New York City got handed some loose change in exchange for a newspaper. In that collection of coins was a nickel. The nickel felt quite light as the boy rummaged through his pocket of cash. Something did not feel right, so the young boy tossed the coin on the hard concrete. On impact, the coin split open and the boy found a tiny photograph inside of the coin. After the paperboy had sold all of his papers, he headed home but met one of his friends on his way. The boy told his friend of what he had discovered that day, and he showed him the picture and the hollow coin. The friend then went home and told his father of what he had just witnessed. The father took great interest in his son's story, who happened to be a policeman. The next morning when the policeman returned to work, the story was related to the higher ups and an investigation started. The photograph revealed 10 columns of numbers, and the detectives knew right away that this was a secret coded message. For the next 4 years, the code could not be broken, and the identity of the source remained a mystery.

It wasn't until 1957 when a Soviet agent named Hayhanen contacted the American Secret Services. He wanted to defect and was willing to share as much secret knowledge that he possessed. With a formal agreement made, Hayhanen had information that he was willing to share, including a small collection of hollow coins that were on his person during his initial interviews. The American detectives were able to connect his hollow coins with the one found by the newspaper boy many years before. It turned out that the message in the hollow coin that was found by the newspaper boy was meant for Hayhanen, who never received it. [31]

[32] / On 26 Oct 1997, at the Circuito Permanente de Jerez

racetrack in Spain, the Formula One auto racing series qualifying session was held on a warm Saturday afternoon. Each driver was allowed up to twelve timed laps, with their fastest lap used to determine their grid position. Cars were timed using a TAG Heuer timing system, which measured to an accuracy of one-thousandth of a second. At the end of the session, the three fastest drivers had all set the same lap time, the first time this had happened in the history of the World Championship. Jacques Villeneuve was first to set a time of 1:21.072, fourteen minutes later, Michael Schumacher posted an identical time. Heinz-Harald Frentzen crossed the line, again with a time of 1:21.072. Under the regulations, in the event of drivers setting equal times in qualifying, Villeneuve was awarded pole position on the starting grid for the race, with Schumacher second and Frentzen third. [32]

[33] / Maarten de Jonge managed to twice cheat death by

simply changing his plane reservations. According to The 29-year-old Dutch athlete who competes for Malaysia's Terengganu Cycling Team was scheduled to fly on Malaysia Airlines Flight 17, which was shot out of the sky on July 17 while en route from Amsterdam to Kuala Lumpur. Seeing there was a cheaper flight later that same day, de Jonge switched. Nearly 300 people on board Flight 17 died when the plane was struck by a surface-to-air missile over Ukraine. Not a few months later De Jonge also planned to travel on the still-missing Malaysia Airlines Flight 370, which disappeared on March 8, presumably over the Indian Ocean. He changed his flight plans to avoid a stopover in Beijing but ended up speaking with several passengers on Flight 370 while waiting for his plane to take off. "I could have taken that one just as easily," de Jonge said in an interview. "It's inconceivable. I am very sorry for the passengers and their families, yet I am very pleased I'm unharmed." That plane, along with its 227 passengers and 12 crew members, as of publishing date, has yet to be found.

[34] / Many years ago, Tommy Lasorda of the LA Dodgers

signed a ball for a friend. He wrote "To Frank, thanks for coming to the game. Best wishes, Tommy Lasorda". Many years later, somehow that ball got lost, put aside and boxed up in someone attic space. When the local baseball league asked for donations from the community, the baseball, with many others were retrieved and donated. The ball ended up a large bucket that was supplied by the little league. After the game was underway and after many pitches were thrown, the ball made its way to the umpire in one of the middle innings. The umpire gave the ball to the pitcher who looked at it and saw there was writing but thought nothing of it. He pitched the ball with was swung on and fouled off into the crowd of parents sitting on the bleachers. A man caught the ball and looked down to see the writing on the ball. Moving the ball in his hands he started to read what was written on the faded ball. Almost causing the man to doubt reality, he read those words once more "To Frank, thanks for coming to the game. Best wishes, Tommy Lasorda", as the man who caught the ball was named Frank. [34]

[35] / In 2007, 23-year-old Stacy Peterson lived in

Bollingbrook, Illinois with her police officer husband, Drew Peterson, who was 30 years older and on his fourth marriage. It was on October 28 of the same year, Stacy went missing. Since her marriage to Drew was troubled due to the age difference, suspicion immediately turned to him.

Back in 2004, Drew's third wife, Kathleen Savio, was found dead in her bathtub in what was initially believed to be an accidental drowning. Drew collected a substantial life insurance policy from the death of his third wife. But due to Stacy's disappearance, this prompted an additional investigation into what was a closed case on Kathleen's drowning. With more evidence showing up and much more advanced police investigation equipment, in 2009 Drew was charged with his ex-wife's murder and was sentenced to 38 years in prison. While in prison, Drew remained the prime suspect in Stacy's disappearance, but her body has never been found.

Stacy's disappearance was just the latest in a long line of family tragedies. Confidence takes full flight when Stacy's 40-year-old mother, Christie Cales, had also disappeared under suspicious circumstances in 2000. Christie had six children but two of them died as infants during the 1980s. Christie abused drugs and alcohol, was often in trouble with the law, and had a turbulent relationship with her husband.

In 1998, Christie was living with her boyfriend in Blue Island, Illinois. On March 11, she apparently walked out of her home and never returned, and that was the last anyone ever saw of her. Much like her daughter, Christie's family has always suspected that her spouse was responsible for her disappearance, but there wasn't enough evidence to charge him. Officially, both Christie Cales and her daughter remain missing.

[36] / On December 6, 1983, an unidentified Hispanic man

was found dead in a vacant lot in Hialeah, Florida from strangulation. For a brief period, this murder became known as the "Liquid Matthew Case" because of a series of bizarre letters and notes discovered at the scene. First of the evidence found was a plastic bag taped behind a nearby "no dumping" sign containing a note with some cryptic poetry. It read:

"Now the motive is clear, and the victim is too. You've got all the answers. Just follow the clues." The poetry also contained a riddle which led police to the next clue. After following the clues, another poem was taped behind a speed limit sign. This poem contained the disturbing verses: "Yes, Matthew is dead, but his body not felt. Those brains were not Matt's because his body did melt. For Billy threw Matthew in some hot boiling oil. To confuse the police for the mystery they did toil." The police had no solid leads, so they took to the airwaves to ask if the public could solve the riddle of the murder.

However, there soon turned out to be an innocent explanation for this confusing murder mystery. Someone from the area of the murder contacted the police to explain the notes that were found. During Halloween, four local churches had organized an elaborate murder mystery game where the participants created fictitious crimes and hid cryptic clues throughout the area. The strange poetry was all part of this murder mystery game. Since it wound up raining on the night the game took place, the notes were never retrieved and remained there for over a month. In a macabre coincidence, a real murder victim was found in the exact same area, but his death ultimately had no connection to the cryptic poetry whatsoever. In the end, the victim was identified as a Colombian seaman named Francisco Patino Gutierrez, and his murder was believed to be related to drug smuggling and not a church game. [36]

[37] / Historical information about Sacagawea is very limited

 which includes folklore mixed with fact. Sacagawea was born into an *Agaidika* (Salmon Eater) of Lemhi Shoshone tribe near Salmon, Idaho, in Lemhi County. In 1800, when she was approximately 12 years old, she and several other girls were kidnapped by a group of Hidatsa in a battle that resulted in the deaths of several Shoshone. She was kept captive at a Hidatsa village near present-day Washburn, North Dakota. At approximately age 13, Sacagawea was sold into a non-consensual "marriage" to Toussaint Charbonneau, a Quebecois trapper living in the village who may have won Sacagawea while gambling.

Sacagawea was pregnant with her first child when the Corps of Discovery arrived near the Hidatsa villages to spend the winter of 1804–05. The Corps of Discovery was led by Captain Meriwether Lewis and Captain William Clark, who with the help of the locals-built Fort Mandan. Fort Mandan was a triangular fort which provided shelter, protection, and a place of cultural interchange between the explorers and the area's Indian inhabitants, for whom the fort was named. Captain Meriwether Lewis and Captain William Clark interviewed several trappers who might be able to interpret or guide the expedition up the Missouri River in the springtime. An agreement was forged to hire

Charbonneau as an interpreter because they discovered his wife spoke Shoshone, and they knew they would need the help of Shoshone tribes at the headwaters of the Missouri.

Clark recorded in his journal on November 4, 1804:

"a French man by Name Chabonah, who Speaks the Big Belley language visit us, he wished to hire & inform us his 2 Squars (squaws) were Snake Indians, we engaged him to go on with us and take one of his wives to interpret the Snake language."

In their exploration of the Western United States in 1804, Lewis and Clark were using Sacagawea as an interpreter with the native people as they traveled west. Before they crossed the Rocky Mountains, they had to secure horses for their journey from the local Indian tribes. The local Indian tribe didn't trust Lewis and Clark and believed they might be part of a war party. As Sacagawea was interpreting and talking with the Indian chief and getting nowhere. As the negotiations continued, Sacagawea started to get a feeling that she may know this person. After asking a few personal questions she suddenly realized that the chief was her long-lost brother. She was taken as a slave from a neighboring tribe at a very young age. It completely changed the direction of the talks and Lewis and Clark's party of 40 people got their horses while Sacagawea got her brother back. [37]

[38] / *January 30, 1835, in the U.S. Capitol building, an*  *armed assailant tried to shoot President Andrew Jackson leading to the first ever assassination attempt made against an American president. Jackson emerged unscathed after the would-be killer's pistols failed to discharge, but the assassination attempt sparked widespread talk of a conspiracy on Capitol Hill.* Jackson was to attend the funeral of South Carolina Representative Warren Davis.

A well-dressed man and a mild-mannered house painter growing increasingly unhinged named Richard Lawrence, waited outside in a crowd that had gathered near the Capitol. He stood with a pair of single-shot brass pistols concealed beneath his cloak.

As the president stepped onto the East Portico, Jackson came face to face with Richard Lawrence, who had emerged from a crowd less than 10 foot away. Without uttering a word, the wild-eyed assassin raised one of his pistols, aimed at the president's heart, and pulled the trigger. The gun's percussion cap erupted with a loud crack, but the shot misfired. Jackson reacted to the danger with startling ferocity. The president raised his walking stick and rushed headlong at the gunman. Lawrence produced a second pistol and fired again, this time at nearly point-blank range. For a second time, the percussion cap erupted, but again the powder failed to explode and launch the bullet. Frontier legend

Davy Crockett, who was then a Congressman tackled Lawrence to the floor and with some help, subdue him.

At the heart of the mystery were Lawrence's guns, which had both misfired against seemingly impossible odds. "The pistols were examined," U.S. Senator Thomas Hart Benton later wrote, "and found to be well loaded; and fired afterward without fail, carrying their bullets true, and driving them through inch boards at thirty feet." Most experts now believe the weather was responsible for saving Jackson's life. Even then, the president was incredibly lucky. The odds of both guns failing were later determined to be 125,000-to-1. [38]

[39] / Henry Ziegland of Honey Grove, Texas, became famous

after it is alleged that he separated from his girlfriend back in 1893. Her brother was so upset that he wanted revenge for his selfish action and proceeded to confront Ziegland and pulled a pistol, discharging a single shot. However, the bullet barely grazed his face before embedding itself in the trunk of a tree. The brother, thinking he had killed Henry in a rage of anger, he placed the same pistol to his own body and pulled the trigger. Twenty years later, in 1913, Ziegland noticed the tree was dying of old age and rot, so he decided to remove the tree from his property. Unable to perform the task with an axe alone, he decided to take drastic measures and use dynamite. Lighting the fuse, he ran back to what he thought was a safe distance, turned and stood proudly as the fuse burned down. The explosion was more than he expected, the explosion ripped the tree apart in millions of splinter size pieces, the bullet, which had originally been intended for Ziegland many years before, became dislodged with such a velocity that it was shot into Ziegland's head, killing him immediately. This story was never fully unverified. [39]

[40] / The creators of *The Simpsons* made an episode back in

the year 2000 which made a joke about Donald Trump becoming president of the United States. Who could ever have guessed that one day it would become a true fact? Even more amazing is the fact that the show presented Trump's election campaign in a way that was almost identical to scenes from real life when he launched his presidential bid. Trump was seen descending an elevator with cheering fans around him in the center of a shopping mall. [40]

[41] / On British television, a show called "The Chase"

has four contestants stood behind pedestals with their names in large letters lit up in lights. The four contestants this week were named Rachael, Ross, Phoebe, and Joe all took part on the ITV quiz show, but fans of the program couldn't help but speculate over the "coincidence" that sprang to mind of millions of viewers. Looking confused, the game show host Jenny Ryan asked the presenter: "Are you meant to be Chandler?" Turning around to see the row of names, Bradley gasped: "Oh I see. I didn't realize that. I'll be Gunther… because we're Gunther get you!" One viewer tweeted: "Remember the cast of Friends? You'll never believe what they look like now #thechase." With an episode to four contestants that all shared names with characters in the sitcom "Friends".

[42] / Well known American actor Frank Morgan played

numerous roles in the iconic film *The Wizard of Oz*. He was a taxi driver in Emerald City, fortune teller Professor Marvel and the Wizard of Oz himself. With the filming preparing to start, the character of Professor Marvel needed a slightly different look than that of what was originally intended, so the MGM's wardrobe department wanted the look to be more down-on-his-luck gentleman instead of the nicer dressed gentleman. So, Frank Morgan and director Victor Fleming went to a local second-hand store just across the street from the studio. Looking around the store, Fleming found and purchased a nice looking but tattered coat which was ideal for the actor to wear in the upcoming scene. While shooting the film and when on a short scene change, Morgan turned a pocket of the coat inside out and incredibly saw the name L. Frank Baum sown into the lining of the coat. L. Frank Baum was the author of *The Wizard of Oz*! Both Baum's widow and the coat's tailor confirmed that the jacket originally belonged to Mr. Baum. The coat was donated years before and had been passed around since that day, making a full circle back to the Wizard of Oz. [42]

[43] / Two women by the names of Barbara Forrest and Mary

Ashford, were both victims of a similar crime committed in the small town of Erdington,

England. The name of the man accused in both their crimes was Thornton, and both Thornton's were eventually acquitted for their crimes!

Both women had been raped and strangled, while their bodies were found 300 yards apart, and both had been found on the same day – May 27, but 157 years apart. One was found in 1817 and the other was discovered in1974. Not content with that being a crazy coincidence, these two women were also twenty-years-old and happened to share the same birthday. Still not satisfied, even more unbelievably, both had just visited a friend that evening, both had changed into a new dress that night, and both had gone to a dance where they supposedly met their killer. [43]

[44] / Dr. Michael Shermer is the founding publisher of

Skeptic magazine, the executive director of the Skeptics Society, and a monthly columnist for Scientific American. Shermer is also the producer and co-host of the 13-hour Fox Family television series *Exploring the Unknown.*

On September 16, 2014, he wrote about an experience that led him to conclude: "We should not shut the doors of perception when they may be opened to us to marvel in the mysterious." His fiancé's belongings were shipped to the United States from Germany, and among them was her grandfather's 1978 transistor radio. She was very close to her grandfather, who died when she was 16 years old. The radio had not worked for many years. As a nice gesture to his future wife, Shermer attempted to fix the radio but he could not get it working again. Placed back in the drawer, the radio was forgotten once more. It continued its silence in the couple's bedroom.

Three months later, in June 2014, Dr. Michael Shermer was wed to Jennifer Graf. After the ceremony that was performed by Shermer's sister, Tina, who was ordained online for the occasion, his new wife asked to talk with him alone. She was feeling lonely, missing her family back in Germany and also wishing her grandfather could have been alive to give her away. The couple walked to the back of the house where they heard music playing, a love song.

They searched in vain for the source of the music, when Jennifer said, "That can't be what I think it is, can it?" with the look of total shock and disbelief, it became clear that it was the transistor radio in the drawer. "My grandfather is here with us," she said, tearfully. "I'm not alone." Shermer's daughter had heard music coming from the radio just before the ceremony started, though the couple had been in the room only moments before without hearing any music at all. The radio continued to work through their wedding night. "Fittingly, it stopped working the next day and has remained silent ever since," Shermer said. [44]

[45] / Victoria Cross recipient Henry Tandey is a legitimate

hero of war and the most highly decorated British Private of the first World War. Tandey enlisted in the Green Howards Regiment of the British Army in 1910. When WWI broke out, he participated in the Battle of Ypres in 1914 and was subsequently wounded at the Battle of the Somme in 1916. After a recovery in the hospital, he was assigned to 3rd Battalion in May of 1917. He was later wounded yet again during the Battle of Passchendaele in November of that year before returning to duty in January of 1918.

As the war was starting to wrap up in August of 1918, he would see action at the 2nd Battle of Cambrai where he dashed across the dreaded no man's land of World War 1 with two others to bomb a German trench. He came back with 20 German prisoners and was awarded the Distinguished Combat Medal as a result. Later, a similar action was performed, and he was awarded the Military Medal.

On September 28th, he freed many trapped men from impending death and for his actions that day, he was awarded the Victoria Cross and became Britain's most decorated Private of World War 1. And were the story to stop there, it would be enough to own its place in the halls of history.

In late 1918, after being wounded in battle, a young Hitler stumbled across the battlefield only to see a British soldier with every opportunity to kill him. With the British soldier recognizing that the wounded man didn't even raise his rifle, he let him pass. The wounded Hitler waved at the British soldier and what seemed like a random act of compassion during a brutal war would be lost to history as one of the common untold stories.

What is beyond a shadow of a doubt is that some British men had the opportunity to kill Hitler in World War I and for whatever reason, he survived. It may very well be that Hitler in his arrogance attempted to tie himself to one of Britain's war heroes from the war by referencing Tandey. [45]

[46] / On August 6 and 9, 1945, the United States detonated

two nuclear bombs over the Japanese cities of Hiroshima and Nagasaki, respectively. The blasts, and the radiation they caused afterward killed nearly 90,000 people. But in 2009, the Japanese government confirmed that there was at least one man who was in each city on the days of the bombings and lived to tell the tale. On August 6, Tsutomu Yamaguchi was in Hiroshima on a business trip. "As I was walking along, I heard the sound of a plane, I looked up into the sky and saw the B-29, and it dropped two parachutes. I was looking up into the sky at them, and suddenly... it was like a flash of magnesium, a great flash in the sky, and I was blown over." By August 9, he had returned home to Nagasaki, only to experience the trauma for the second time. Despite the double radiation exposure, Yamaguchi lived to be 93. He passed away in 2010 from stomach cancer. [46]

Peoples Personal Stories.

Mickey said: About 20 years ago some friends and I rented an airplane and flew to Martha's Vineyard. There we rented some bikes and rode around all day, stopping at beaches and swimming occasionally, finally ending up at a restaurant. We slept under the airplane and flew back the next day. Years later I was at MIT for a reunion and they had an art show, showing off photography from students. One of the winners was a picture of four biked leaned against each other on a deserted beach with clothing piled on each one. I looked more closely - and they were the bikes we had rented on Martha's Vineyard, with our clothing on the back.

Debbie wrote, "My dad was visiting our summer house (he lives about 500 miles away). It was windy one day and this random guy who was kayaking decided to come ashore and set up camp on the beach. We went and talked to the fella and offered him to stay at our guest house. Turns out this guy lives in the apartment under my father and had paddled the whole 500 miles. The cool thing is that my dad (he is in a wheelchair) is having trouble getting snow and ice off his car in the winter months but for the last two winters his car was mostly snow and ice free in the mornings. The father had no idea who was cleaning off his car. It turns out this guy was taking care of that every time he was doing it to his own car."

April from Australia wrote: "Some years ago my brother- in law, who lived some 5 km away, was visiting my house. His car was stolen right out from under his nose. The brother in law was upset but said that he was getting rid of the car anyhow due to the fact that the car was having serious engine problems. Still upset at the fact that someone stole the car, he sat at the kitchen table with April. We heard the loud sound of a Volkswagen car coming into my street, sputtering and then going very quiet. We looked out of the front door to see that it was, in fact, my brother in law's car being abandoned by would-be thieves, breaking down right in front of my house."

Robert from Ireland wrote: "A show on BBC2 a few years ago told the story about the auto repair guy who was walking past a phone box in the middle of nowhere when the phone began to ring. On a whim, he answered, and was amazed to find he was talking to his dispatcher. She had meant to ring his cell phone but had rung his staff number instead - which happened to be the phone number of the phone he was walking past. I thought that was pretty weird."

As the years move on past 9-11-01, more conspiracy theory, The Project for a New American Century (PNAC) was a neo-con think tank stacked with members such as President George W. Bush's entourage including Dick Cheney, Jeb Bush, Paul Wolfowitz, Donald Rumsfeld, Scooter Libby and Richard Perle. Post-September 11, the four horsemen of PNAC (Cheney, Wolfowitz, Libby and Perle) were the main catalysts for moving into Iraq despite no WMDs. Is it all just a coincidence that the policy they advocated was fulfilled after only a year of power?

Susan Ginsberg of the National Commission on Terrorist Attacks, she stated that three passports were found at the plane crash sites: two in Pennsylvania and one in New York. Another passport was found in a piece of Mohammad Atta's "left-behind luggage."

This is odd because a fireball 100 stories high in a building that collapses to dust and debris leaves behind a perfect passport of one of the culprits to a crime, but it doesn't leave behind the indestructible black boxes of the aircraft recorders. All other passports were burnt or destroyed.

While the rest of the country uses identification to board flights (State IDs for domestic travel, passports for international and non-American's must provide either Green Cards or Passports), a foreign terrorist hijacker was able to board a flight while leaving his passport in his friend's luggage. And that luggage also happened to name all 19 hijackers and their precise motives in carrying out the attacks on the morning of their deaths. Coincidence or conspiracy?

Myfivebest.com state that Steel Framed Buildings – In over 100 years of buildings having steel frames, only 3 have ever collapsed due to fire. The three buildings were all leased by the same man, and all three buildings collapsed in the exact same way. The three buildings I'm referring to are the Twin Towers, and 7 WTC (building nearby that collapsed from damage inflicted by the other buildings). Strange coincidence or that man was in on it too

As the author, I feel this story is the most outrageous of all. Here is how it goes: Wingdings – Some say that Q33NY is the registration number of the first plane to hit the Twin Towers. This has since been proven a hoax, but it is still kind of creepy if you type Q33NY (all caps) in Microsoft Word and then change the font to Wingdings. You can also type in all caps NYPD, and you will have a strange finding. IRAQ WAR is another that could have some significance.

Christopher recounts: I went to a friend's birthday party a couple months back. She had requested that I bring a baseball bat for a piñata that was going to be broken open during the party. I also bought a cake from a local bakery near my apartment. Fast

forward to the end of the party. I'm leaving and it's 1:30 a.m. in the sketchy side of town. I walked to the door, grabbed my leather jacket from the coat rack and put it on over the hoodie I was wearing. I grabbed my bat, the half-eaten cake and left for a tired drive home. This is where things get weird.

I walk out her front door with this big baseball bat slung over my shoulder, cake in hand. I turn left to walk to my car, which is parked down the street when I notice someone is walking parallel to me on the other side of the road. He was going in the same direction, at the same exact pace. This guy is identical to me. He is wearing a leather jacket over a hoodie, with a big baseball bat slung over his shoulder. The only difference between us is that he is wearing a masquerade mask. We both look up and catch each other's eyes. Immediately, the two of us look away to concurrently stare at the ground in disbelief. I am coming from a birthday party, and he looks to have just committed some sort of felonious crime. He looks up, I look away. I look up, he looks away. Finally, we catch eyes for the second time. We stare. We each hold our respective gazes for 20 feet, but it felt like a mile. Now I can't take it anymore. I have to say something. … I blurt out the only thing I can think of: 'Well, this is definitely the craziest coincidence that's happened in my life.' He says nothing, but after a tense second, nods in agreement. He splits down a side street and I get to my car, still in disbelief. I toss my bat and cake into the trunk of my car, and not a second after I close the lid, three cop cars come tearing around the corner. Two goes screaming past me and the third one rolls down his window. Before he can say anything, I blurt out: 'Are you looking for a man in a leather jacket wearing a masquerade mask and carrying a baseball bat?'

The cop says 'yes,' to which I reply, 'He went that way!' and point down the side street.

Finally, arriving home after the long night, I had a realization: What if I had left my friend's apartment 30 seconds later than I did? I would have been the guy, in the leather jacket, with the baseball bat walking down the street at 1:30 a.m. in the morning."

Tyler recounts: It was 2008, I was at a party on the 4th of July. He lived on the top story of a condo block. Everyone is on the balcony drinking and having a good time. I look down and watch as this strange man comes through the gate and up the stairs to where everyone is partying.

When the middle-aged man makes his way to the top and stops everyone to announce, 'I am Muhammad Ali, I come-ah from space mon.' He then sits down, pulls out a bottle of wine from his jacket, and starts drinking. He tells us he came from Africa through space. Obviously, no one believed him, and everyone avoided him, he pulls out a passport from Nigeria and made sure everyone saw it. To the dismay of all the party-goers, he stayed for most of the night. About three years later, while walking back from the store, my roommates and I share the story once more and discuss how bizarre it was. We get back to the house, and as I am walking up the stairs of the porch I get to the, 'I am Muhammad Ali, I come-ah from space mon' part.

I hear from the opposite side of the street, 'No, I am Muhammad Ali mon!'

With a total shock, the same guy walks across the street and sits down on our porch. He pulls out a bottle of wine and starts drinking. All of us were too stunned to react appropriately. To summarize, strange foreigner crashes the party, I summon him like Beetlejuice three years later. He has never been seen since.

Tammy recalls the following:
"One night my 5-year-old daughter, got into bed with me. After both of us going back to sleep, I had a terrible nightmare where I was a murderer. I woke up in the morning and was thinking about my dream when my daughter woke up and looked at me and said, 'Mummy I had a dream that you were killing people."

Lemmy said: In 1982 I traveled to the Glastonbury Music Festival in England I arrived very late on Thursday night after a car breakdown on the way to the gig. Once I found my group of friends I wandered around the grounds. The highlight to that point was when we helped a very ill kid to the medical center, I expect he had way too many beers that day. My day got much better as when I was on my way back to our campsite, I saw something on the ground. Reaching down, I picked up what looked like a folded piece of paper, only to find out it was a roll of banknotes tied with an elastic band. I pocketed it with the intent to hand it in the next morning. In the morning I located another group of friends from my former hometown, including my best friend from school. He looked very unhappy, and on asking him he was so upset? He said that he had lost £100 on the previous evening. I asked him how much and what it looked like. He described the roll of banknotes tied with an elastic band, which I then produced from my pocket and handed over to him. Yes, it's unlikely, but not beyond possibility!

Lance stated: When I was about 12 years old, I had stolen a distant friend's Gameboy game. I ran into my bedroom and locked myself in while he tried to batter the door down. In an act of revenge for actions taken earlier, I deleted his Pokemon save. Being more of a friend of my cousin, I've met him 3-4 times since. My girlfriend mentioned losing her levels on the Xbox, so I told her the story of how I made Joe cry by deleting his levels and how I felt mean really because he must have spent actual weeks getting it to level 80. Then, as I was halfway through my last sentence, Joe messages me on Facebook for the first time in a year or so and says, "Pokémon killer!". It was the weirdest moment of my life and I was a bit scared I had my webcam on broadcast or something.

Bob (if that is his real name) wrote: When traveling in New Zealand in 1996 I stayed at a remote and near empty backpacking hostel. Bored one evening I begged the landlord to open up the outdoor spa for a soak, supported by another lonely traveler.

Finally agreeing, the spa was turned on and I lowered myself in the warm water. Joined by the other traveler, we got to talking about silly things that randomly came to mind. One topic was who and what really annoyed us. I began to talk about one person I found unbearable at school, who'd ended up following me to university. I'd never much thought of him since leaving college but began to warm to my topic, describing how he may be the only person I've ever met I'd happily never want to see ever again. The conversation started to get into more details about this person. The girl asked where he lived and what school he attended. It turned out that my bathing companion on the other side of the world was his girlfriend's cousin.

Andy wrote: In the late 1990s I worked as a mastering engineer in a low-rent recording and mastering studio. It was the days when access to a CD writer was a special thing and this brand-new technology was in high demand. I had the original vinyl recording of Philip Glass' "Einstein On the Beach" Opera and did not want to play it too much more, so decided to transfer it to a CD disc. While assisting a freelance sound engineer recording a band in the studio next door. I had never met this engineer before, he was a bit older than me and worked at much better gigs than I did. The music he was working on could be described as "chanson". While fine-tuning the master sound before writing to CD, replaying segments loudly, the freelance engineer poked his head around the door and gave a start. He then took his shirt off and under the shirt, he wore the limited-edition T-Shirt printed for the premiere of that Opera in that country, a momentous occasion several years earlier. It turned out that he had been the sound engineer at the live event which was the biggest step in his career. He said that he rarely wore the T-Shirt because it was so special. He could not recall what made him chose it for that day, but of course, he had not expected to hear the music at our studio. I reckon one needs to know more about the market for sound engineers in the late 90s, Philip Glass music, the cultural clash of the Glass opera and our studio environment, and the lovingly preserved T-Shirt to understand both of our surprise. Or maybe we were just kidding ourselves. But it was a bit spooky. (Nevertheless, we both remained completely rational people.)

Colin recalled: I used to have an electronic archiving company. Our first client in 1999 was The Battle of Britain Memorial Flight at RAF Coningsby for whom we scanned many thousands of Warbird drawings. In September 1999 we decided to scan a copy of the Daily Telegraph to demonstrate the power of our software (which could find any page using keyword searches). I volunteered to bring in an old edition which I'd kept from the day my son was born (15/4/1983). By a strange coincidence, the front page of that edition carried a story about Ray Hannah who had just paid a lot of money for a Spitfire. But the spooky thing was that when I bought the Telegraph that day (27/9/1999), the front page carried an article about Mr. Hannah's son, Mark who had died in a

Spitfire accident that weekend. The hairs on the back of my neck still stand up when I remember this.

Quick Notes

- Napoleon and Hitler were born 129 years apart. They came to power 129 years apart. They declared war on Russia 129 years apart and both were defeated 129 years apart.

- During the building of the Hoover Dam, 112 men died during the construction. The first to die was on Dec 20, 1922, a man named J.G. Tierney. 13 years later, on the same date, Dec 20, 1935, the last man was to die. His name was Patrick Tierney, Patrick was the son of J.G. Tierney, the first to die.

- In 1895, there were only two cars in the state of Ohio. They managed to run into each other causing so much damage, both cars were classed as a write-off, leaving no cars running and operating in the Buckeye State.

- In 2000, during the production of the video game "Deus Ex" developed by Ion Storm and published by Eidos Interactive, was a glaring mistake made in production. With the video game manufactured, it was noticed that during the clips of the New York skyline, someone had forgotten to add the World Trade Center's Twin Towers. With it being too late to pull all the copies of the game that was being manufactured. The game designers decided to make a public statement with an additional storyline for the missing buildings. They would use a storyline to say that this video game was based on the future and the Twin Towers were destroyed in a terrorist attack.

• Olaf Stapledon wrote a science fiction novel called "Last and First Man" in 1930 which describes Italy being overrun by a dictator named Mussolini who was defeated in war and murdered in the streets. It also describes a European Union being formed after the war and America and China becoming the two greatest superpowers of the world. This story clearly came true as Benito Mussolini, the deposed Italian fascist dictator, occurred on 28 April 1945, in the final days of World War II in Europe, when he was summarily executed by Italian partisans in the small village of Giulino di Mezzegra in northern Italy. It is also known that China and the USA grew to be World power.

• Lincoln - Kennedy coincidences

Lincoln was elected in 1860, Kennedy in 1960, 100 years apart Both men were deeply involved in civil rights for African Americans. Both men were assassinated on a Friday, in the presence of their wives.

Both men were succeeded by vice-presidents named Johnson who were southern Democrats and former senators. Andrew Johnson was born in 1808. Lyndon Johnson was born in 1908, exactly one hundred years later. The first name of Lincoln's private secretary was John, the last name of Kennedy's private secretary was Lincoln.

John Wilkes Booth was born in 1839 while according to some sources, Lee Harvey Oswald was born in 1939, one hundred years later.

Each wife had lost a child while living at the White House. Both men were killed by a bullet that entered the head from behind. Lincoln was killed in Ford's Theater. Kennedy met his death while riding in a Lincoln convertible made by the Ford Motor Company.

Both assassins were Southerners who held extremist views. Both assassins were murdered before they could be brought to trial. Booth shot Lincoln in a theater and fled to a warehouse. Oswald shot Kennedy from a warehouse and fled to a theater. A Lincoln staffer Miss Kennedy told him not to go to the Theater. A Kennedy staffer Miss Lincoln told him not to go to Dallas.

- In 1953, television reporter Irv Kupcinet was in London to cover the coronation of Elizabeth II. In one of the drawers in his room at the Savoy Hotel, he found some items that, by their identification, belonged to a man named Harry Hannin. Harry Hannin was a basketball star with the famed Harlem Globetrotters was a good friend of Kupcinet's. But the story has yet another twist to it. Just two days later, and before he could tell Hannin of his lucky discovery, Kupcinet received a letter from Hannin. In the letter, Hannin told Kupcinet that while staying at the Hotel Meurice in Paris, he found in a drawer a tie – with Kupcinet's name on it.

- An American writer Anne Parrish and her husband were on vacation in Paris in 1920. They were browsing the areas bookshops, and Anne picked up a book that was a favorite of hers entitled, "Jack Frost and Other Stories." Anne told her husband that she had been given a copy as a child by her parents and had wonderful memories of the book. Anne's husband took the book and opened it. On the inside cover, there was a handwritten inscription. It said,

"Anne Parrish, 209 N Weber Street, Colorado Springs".
The inscription was written in Anne's handwriting. It was
Anne's very own book from all those years ago!

- In 1914 a woman from Strasbourg, Germany took her son
  to be photographed for his family portrait. Before digital
  and roll film, she would have bought a film plate, and after
  the photo was taken said she would return in a few days
  when the portrait was developed. It was poor timing as
  World War I broke out that next day, and she was not able
  to collect the photo. Two years later she was now living in
  Frankfurt Germany and gave birth to a daughter. She was
  still disappointed because she still didn't have any photos
  of her children, so she once again bought a film plate and
  another photo was taken, this time of her daughter. When
  the new photo plate was developed it turned out to be
  a double exposure. Her daughter's image was
  superimposed on the earlier picture of her son. Incredibly
  her original film plate was never developed and had
  somehow ended up in Frankfurt 100 miles away. She
  bought the same plate with the original photo still on it.

- Were the hijackers lucky on 9/11 or had an insider tipped
  them off? That morning, most of the eastern air defense of
  NORAD was preoccupied with a war game that left many
  jets far away from Washington and New York. In the first

phone call between the air-traffic controller and NORAD, the first question out of the NORAD employee's mouth is, "Is this real world or exercise?" On July 7, 2005, the day of the London Bombings, London police were also running a simulated exercise: by a stroke of amazing coincidence that exercises revolved around a terrorist bombing in the London subways. Further, Mayor Guiliani happened to be in London advising on security.

- In 1973, actor Anthony Hopkins agreed to appear in "The Girl from Petrovka", based on a novel by George Feifer. Unable to find a copy of the book anywhere he wandered the streets, not knowing what to do. Hopkins decided he was out of luck and returned to the train station. As he took a seat on a bench while waiting for his train to arrive, he noticed a book laying on the bench. There lied a copy of the book he was looking for. This book was annotated (personal) copy, which Feifer had lent to a friend, and which had been stolen from his friend's car.

- Carl Jung said that a young woman I was treating had, at a critical moment, a dream in which she was given a golden scarab. While she was telling this dream, I sat with my back to a window. Suddenly I heard a noise behind me, like a gentle tapping. I turned around and saw a flying insect knocking against the window-pane from outside. I opened the window and caught the creature in the air as it flew in. It was the nearest analogy to the golden scarab that one finds in our latitudes, a scarabaei beetle, which contrary to its usual habits had evidently felt an urge to get into a dark room at this moment. I must admit that nothing like it ever happened to me before or since and that the dream of the patient has remained unique in my experience."

- In 2002, two 70-year-old twin brothers died two hours apart, and that's not the eerie part. The first brother was riding his bike on a roadway north of Helsinki when he was hit by a truck and killed. Before the family was even informed of his death, the second brother also died. He was riding his bike when he was hit by a truck and killed. The accidents happened on the same road, less than a mile apart, and the BBC quoted one of the Finnish police officers involved in the cases as saying, "This is simply a historical coincidence. Although the road is a busy one, accidents don't occur every day. It made my hair stand on end when I heard the two were brothers and identical twins at that.

- In the 1930's Joseph Figlock was walking down the street in Detroit. A mother's baby fell from a high window onto Figlock who was passing below. The baby's fall was broken and both man and baby were unharmed. A stroke of luck on its own, but a year later, the very same baby fell from the very same window onto poor, unsuspecting Joseph Figlock as he was again passing beneath. And again, they both survived the event."

- This story is of identical twins born in Ohio. The twin boys were separated at birth, being adopted by different families. Unknown to each other, both families named the boys James. Both James grew up not even knowing of the other, yet both sought law-enforcement training, both skilled in mechanical drawing and carpentry, and each had married women named Linda. They both had sons whom one named James Alan and the other named James Allan. The twins divorced their wives and married other women – both named Betty. And they both owned a dog named Toy. Forty years after their childhood separation, the two men were reunited to share their amazingly similar lives.

- John and Arthur Mowforth were twins who lived about 80 miles apart in England. On the evening of May 22, 1975, both men fell ill from chest pains. The families of both men were completely unaware of the other's illness. Both men were rushed to separate hospitals at approximately the same time. And both died of heart attacks shortly after arrival.

- The movie, "Game of Death" is based on a story that has Bruce Lee playing an actor in the film. The climactic scene in the movie comes when Lee's character is shot using a prop gun that turns out to be loaded, whilst shooting The Crow, Lee's son, Brandon, was accidentally killed when a prop gun mistakenly fired.

- Composer George Handel was a neighbor of famous guitarist Jimi Hendrix separated by two centuries. Handel lived in London at 25 Brook Street, whilst Hendrix lived for a time at 23 Brook Street. They were both incredible musicians who had a major influence on the development of music in their respective eras.

- Actress, Anne Hathaway's husband, Adam Shulman, has an uncanny resemblance to William Shakespeare. William Shakespeare's wife was also named Anne Hathaway.

- An Australian man named Bill Morgan was declared dead for 14 minutes and was revived. To celebrate his survival, he bought a scratch card and won a $27,000 car. The news reporter asked him to reenact the scratch card moment to capture it on camera, so he bought another card and won a $250,000 jackpot in it.

- A first-time journalist named Stephen Diamond arrived in San Francisco with only $10 to his name. He couldn't even afford a notepad to write on, yet he surged ahead using whatever paper he could find. He was tempted to steal a notepad but thought better of it. Then he saw just what he needed, "a pad of paper, face-down on top of a pile of trash, clothes, shoes, old books." Turning over the pad he was delighted to see the header on this notepad. It said "Stephen Diamond, M.D." What were the chances of Diamond finding a notepad with his name on it in pristine condition in the trash just when he needed it most? He later went on to write the cult classic "What the Trees Said."

- A poker player Robert Fallon was shot by an upset opponent back in 1858. The body was quickly removed and Fallon place at the table was cleared but the winnings lay still on the table. No other player wanted to sit in "an unfortunate place." However, the game had to go on, and the rivals had a quick word came out of the saloon out and soon returned with a young man who happened to be passing by on the street. The young man takes his seat at the table and he was handed $ 600, which was the dead man's winnings. All the money was placed as an initial bet. The young man went on to win much more that night.

After the police had analyzed the situation and arresting the main suspects in the murder of Robert Fallon, the police ordered the transfer of $600 won by the deceased, his next of kin, which turned out to be all the same successful young player, who has not seen his father for more than 7 years and had no idea he was replacing his dead father!

- In 1975, while riding a moped on the island of Bermuda, a man was struck and killed by a taxi. Exactly one year later, this man's brother was killed in the very same way when riding a moped. It was established that he was, in fact, riding the very same moped. To make this coincidence even more difficult to believe, he was struck by the very same taxi driven by the same driver who, wait for it, was even carrying the very same passenger.

- We are lucky to be able to witness eclipses of the sun. They are rare, but we do not know how lucky we really are. The reason is that the sun and moon appear to be the same size because of an astonishing coincidence. The moon is 400 times smaller but 400 times closer, which makes the eclipses possible. Also, complete eclipses won't be possible forever as the moon is slowly drifting away from Earth.

- Back in 1980, a woman named Maureen Wilcox played the Rhode Island and the Massachusetts lotteries at the same time on the same day. She hit the correct numbers for both lotteries. Unfortunately, she picked all the correct Massachusetts numbers on her Rhode Island ticket and all the right Rhode Island numbers on her Massachusetts ticket. That is worse than getting no numbers at all or missing out by one number.

- In consecutive lottery games in 2009, the Bulgarian National lottery randomly picked the same set of six winning numbers. Naturally, some people suspected fraud. The math will show that it 43 years for there to exist a better than even chance for the same sets of numbers to get drawn.

- British Army officer, Major Summerford, was fighting in World War I, when Summerford was knocked off his horse by a flash of lightning and paralyzed from the waist down. Summerford retired and moved to Vancouver, Canada. Many years later in 1924, Summerford was fishing alongside a river when lightning hit the tree where he was sitting, and once more, he was paralyzed in his right side. Six years later, he was out walking on a summer's day when a lightning bolt smashed into him, permanently paralyzing him. He died two years later after complications from his injuries. Thinking this was the end of the story, you are wrong. Four years later, during a storm by an amazing coincidence, lightning struck a cemetery and destroyed his tombstone.

- Claude Volbonne killed Baron Rodemire de Tarazone of France in 1872. 21 years earlier, the Baron's father had been murdered by someone else called Claude Volbonne.

- In November of 1911, three men were hanged at Greenberry Hill in London after being convicted of the murder of Sir Edmund Berry. As a strange coincidence, their names were Green, Berry, and Hill.

- Oregon's Columbian newspaper announced the winning Pick 4 lottery numbers for June 28, 2000, in advance. The newspaper had intended to print the previous set of winning numbers but mistakenly printed those for the state of Virginia, namely 6-8-5-5. By a strange coincidence, in the next Oregon lottery, those same numbers were drawn.

- John Lyne could well be Britain's unluckiest man. 'Calamity John' has suffered 16 major accidents in his life, including lightning strikes, a rock-fall in a mine and three car crashes. 'I don't think there is any reason or explanation. Things could have been much worse, and I could have died but it doesn't worry me too much. John Lyne's mishaps covered his entire life and he has even been known to suffer two accidents at once. As a child, he fell off a horse, only to be run over by a delivery van. When he was a teenager, he broke his arm falling from a tree and on his way back from the hospital, his bus crashed, breaking the same arm in another place. The date, of course, was Friday the 13th.

- At just three months old, Rose Davies of Gwent Wales had been given up for adoption by her mother. She was taken in by a foster family and as she grew, discovered she had three long lost brothers. She easily found brothers Sid and John, but there was no trace of younger brother Chris. In a strange twist, she found Chris and his family lived right across the street from her and at the time she discovered they were related, she had already known him for three months. It turns out Chris had been searching for his big sister too!

- A computer error gave two American women named Patricia Ann Campbell the same Social Security number. The ladies were asked to meet up to rectify the error. While waiting for an official to come into the room the two ladies made a few more similar discoveries. In addition to having the same name, both were born on March 13, 1941. Both of their dads were named Robert Campbell. Both got married to men who served in the military in 1959 and had two children, aged 19 and 21. Both had studied cosmetics, worked as book-keepers and both were even interested in oil painting.

- A ship sank off the coast of Wales on December 5, 1664. All 81 passengers died, except one. His name was Hugh Williams. Then on December 5th, 1785 another ship with

60 aboard sank in the same location. The only survivor – a man named Hugh Williams. In 1820 on December 5th, a third vessel sank in the Menai Strait. All 25 aboard were drowned except, you guessed it, a man named Hugh Williams. One version of the story appears as a footnote on page 155 of Cliffe's Book of North Wales, published in 1851. The story starts out the same with the sinking on December 5, 1664, and 1785, with Hugh Williams, the only survivor. The story changes for the 1820 sinking. Hugh Williams is still the sole survivor, but the sinking took place on August 5th, not December 5th. The footnote goes on to mention that, *"Again on May 20th, 1842, a boat was crossing the Menai, near the spot where the above catastrophes happened, when she upset with 15 passengers, and all perished save one; but in this instance, the name of the survivor was Richard Thomas."* So, the facts show that this is not a coincidence more than a sea story or wives tale?

- Movie actor and director, Adam Sandler's characters almost always have a name that ends in a "y" sound. Billy, Happy, Robbie, Sonny, Nicky, Davey, Whitey, etc., etc. Not only that, nearly all of the female love interests in his films have names that start with "V": Veronica Vaughn, Virginia Vennet, Vicki Vallencurt, Vanessa, Valerie Veran, etc.

- In 1899 a bolt of lightning killed a man as he stood in his backyard in Italy. Thirty years later his son was killed in the **same way and in the same place.** On October 8, 1949, Rolla Primarda, the grandson of the first victim and the son of the second, became the third victim.

- Joseph Stalin wanted to see the face of the 14th-century Turko-Mongol warlord Tamerlane entombed in Samarkand. Legend held that "the War God's sleep must not be disturbed," If Tamerlane's corpse were disturbed, Tamerlane would return on the third day, bringing a war to the ones that disturbed him. Stalin scoffed at the legend and on June 19, 1941, he opened the coffin. On June 21, Stalin found out Germany was set to invade the Soviet Union at dawn the next day.

- On Friday, Aug. 13, 2010, a 13-year-old boy was struck by lightning at 13:13 (1:13 p.m.) in Suffolk, England. Rex Clarke, a St. John Ambulance team leader, said, "Suddenly there was this huge crack of lightning really close to the seafront and really loud thunder. Seconds later we got a call someone had been hit. The boy was breathing and was conscious." The boy only suffered a small burn on his body. "It's all a bit strange that he was 13, and it happened at 13:13 on Friday 13."

- In the 1930s, Warner Brothers were pressured by FDR's Attorney General Homer Cummings to make a series of films that glorified law enforcement agents rather than criminal, as they had made many popular gangster films to that points. So, it was then that Warner Bros decided to make a series of Secret Service films starring actor Ronald Reagan. Reagan once called one of the movies, *Code of the Secret Service*, "the worst picture I ever made," but the movie saved his life. Over 40 years later, President Reagan was the target of an assassination attempt, but his life was spared thanks to quick thinking by Secret Service Agent Jerry Parr. The weird part? Parr was inspired to join the Secret Service after watching Ronald Reagan in *Code of the Secret Service*.

- *The Matrix movie* featured one of the eeriest 9/11 coincidences. In the first movie (originally released in 1999), Neo's passport expires on September 11th, 2001.

- Chuck Willis' last chart single was "What Am I Living For" b/w "Hang Up My Rock & Roll Shoes". A short while after it was released, he died of peritonitis.

- Charles M. Schulz of "Peanuts" fame died the night before his last strip was published.

- The song "Blame it on the boogie" is a major hit for The Jacksons. People could easily believe this was an original written by them. But The Jacksons didn't write it, it's of a song previously released and written by a German composer whose name is Mickael Jackson.

- A blurry photo of a man stealing a wallet in a store ran on the bottom of the front page of Idaho's Lewiston Tribune. Above it was an unrelated photo of a man painting a business. Readers noticed both men were wearing the same clothes and could be the same man. He was, leading to his arrest.

- On the evening of Orson Welles' famous War of the Worlds broadcast there was a factory that caught fire in New Jersey, so when people listening to the story in New York looked over to Jersey they saw plumes of smoke on the horizon, leading to "eyewitness accounts" of the alien invasion.

Citations:

[1] https://marktwainhouse.org

[2] http://newsfeed.time.com

[3] http://rogerjnorton.com

[4] https://www.biography.com

[5] https://en.wikipedia.org

[6] https://www.warhistoryonline.com

[7] http://www.beliefnet.com

[8] http://rogerjnorton.com

[9] https://www.history.com

[10] http://www.dailymail.co.uk/news/article-3254422

[11] https://en.wikipedia.org/wiki/Wilmer_McLean

[12] https://fr.wikipedia.org

[13] https://www.mirror.co.uk

[14] http://www.slemen.com

[15] http://anomalyinfo.com

[16] http://www.texasescapes.com

[17] https://www.history.com

[18] https://en.wikinews.org

[19] http://www.grunge.com

[20] https://doyouremember.com

[21] http://www.ssqq.com

[22] http://listverse.com

[23] https://en.wikipedia.org/wiki/Daniel_du_Toit

[24] /National Archives Office of Strategy and Communications staff writer Rob Crotty.

[25] / https://prologue.blogs.archives.gov

[26] / https://www.theepochtimes.com

[27] / http://whatculture.com

[28] / http://whatculture.com

[29] / http://www.nairaland.com

[30] / http://www.check-six.com

[31] / http://www.ourlittleearth.com

[32] / https://en.wikipedia.org/wiki/1997_European_Grand_Prix

[33] / http://www.dailymail.co.uk

[34] / https://www.reddit.com

[35] / http://listverse.com

[36] / http://thuglifer.com

[37] / https://www.revolvy.com

[38] / https://www.history.com

[39] / https://findery.com

[40] / http://www.dailymail.co.uk

[41] / https://www.thesun.co.uk

[42] / http://eberesamuel.blogspot.com

[43] / http://eberesamuel.blogspot.com

[44] / http://www.theepochtimes.com

[45] / https://www.warhistoryonline.com

[46] / https://www.ibtimes.co.uk

Also Contributing:

http://www.guy-sports.com

https://www.scientificamerican.com

https://www.oddee.com/item_99043.aspx

https://www.express.co.uk/showbiz/tv-radio/778696/

https://www.snopes.com

http://www.hollywood.com

http://www.forums.stevehoffman.tv

https://understandinguncertainty.org

https://www.ripleys.com

Printed in Great Britain
by Amazon